A Visual Guide to

Financial Statements

Overview for Non-Financial Managers & Investors

Thomas R. Ittelson

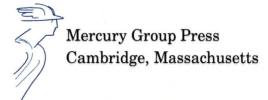

Mercury Group Press
Cambridge, Massachusetts

Available in quantity from the publisher.

ISBN: 978-0-9971089-7-2 *(paperback)*
ISBN: 978-1-970050-00-4 *(hardcover)*
ISBN: 978-1-970050-02-8 *(Amazon Kindle eBook)*
ISBN: 978-1-970050-03-5 *(Apple iBook)*

 **Mercury Group Press**
P.O. Box 381350
Cambridge, MA 02238
www.mercurygrouppress.com
info@mercurygroup.com
617-285-1168

Publisher's Cataloging-in-Publishing Data

Names: Ittelson, Thomas R., 1946- author.

Title: Visial guide to financial statements : overview for non-financial managers & investors / Thomas R. Ittelson.

Description: Cambridge, Massachusetts : Mercury Group Press, [2019] | Includes glossary and index.

Identifiers: ISBN: 978-0-9971089-7-2 (paperback) | 978-1-970050-02-8 (Amazon Kindle) | 978-1-970050-03-5 (Apple iBook) 978-1-970050-00-4 (hardcover)

Subjects: LCSH: Financial statements--Handbooks, manuals, etc. | Financial statements--Study and teaching. | Corporations--Finance--Handbooks, manuals, etc. | Corporations--Accounting-- Handbooks, manuals, etc. | Accounting--Handbooks, manuals, etc. | Bookkeeping--Handbooks, manuals, etc. | Cash flow--Handbooks, manuals, etc. | Ratio analysis--Handbooks, manuals, etc. | BISAC: BUSINESS & ECONOMICS / Accounting / Financial.

Classification: LCC: HF5681.B2 I746 2019 | DDC: 657/.3--dc23

Contents

Other books by Thomas R. Ittelson:

Financial Statements: Step-by-Step Guide to Understanding and Creating Financial Reports, Second Edition Career Press, 2009 (285 pages)
    ISBN: 978-1-60163-023-0 (paperback)
    ASIN: B004GGU342 (Kindle eBook)

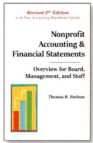

Nonprofit Accounting & Financial Statements: Overview for Board, Management, and Staff Mercury Group Press, 2017 (230 pages)
    ISBN: 978-0-9971089-6-5 (paperback)
    ASIN: B075W21J3F (Kindle eBook)

Picture Book of Nonprofit Financial Statements
Mercury Group Press, 2017 (70 pages)
    ISBN: 978-0-9971089-4-1 (paperback)
    ASIN: B072Q4KXDQ (Kindle eBook)

"And this is our department of experimental accounting."

Preface

Accounting is the "language of business." A company's financial statements — the topic of this book — are the summary communications to its owners (and the taxing government) of its accounting information: its sales, costs, expenses, profits, assets, and liabilities.

Businesses exist to make a profit. Financial statements describe numerically how the profit is made. Businesses own things and owe things. Financial statements show what and how much.

Accounting rules help to ensure that financial information is understandable and comparable to that of other companies and that all companies operate to an acceptable minimum standard of ethics.

Non-Financial Managers

One goal in my writing this book is to help non-financial folks — salespeople, researchers, engineers, manufacturing folks, HR staff, and the like — appreciate the numbers of business. Such an understanding should make you better able to do your jobs, or at least better appreciate what makes for good business performance. Perhaps this book will make your job more fun too!

Writing for the novice, I translate the morass of detailed accounting numbers into pictures that are both simple and elegant, if not actually delicious. The 40 pages in this book will give you all you need to understand how your business is doing and to be able to explain it to others in plain English. I do recommend having cookies or a slice of pie available while reading. Just saying.

Investors

Ultimately, good financial performance drives investment value and stock price. Financial statements document that performance for all to see. Financial statements are the primary tool that company's use to communicate that performance—good or bad—to investors and other sources of capital (think banks) that companies need to court.

To be a savvy investor, I think you must understand financial statement reporting. This book's easy to read format should benefit investors, most of whom do not have a financial background.

I have also written a much more detailed 285-page accounting textbook published by Career Press: *Financial Statements: Step-by-Step Guide to Understanding and Creating Financial Reports* (ISBN: 978-1-60163-023-0). Currently in its 2nd edition, with over 200,000 copies in print, this book is popular as a secondary text in both undergraduate accounting and business school finance classes. As with this picture book, no previous accounting knowledge is required. Read both!

See the Index & Glossary at the back of this book, for web references and other good stuff. You can understand financial statements. You can learn the language; you can learn the structure. Have a cookie.

> "**If you can read a nutrition label or a baseball box score, you can understand basic financial statements. If you can follow recipes or apply for a loan, you can learn basic accounting. The basics are not difficult and they are not rocket science.**
>
> **Just as a CPR class teaches you how to perform the basics of cardiac pulmonary resuscitation, this brochure will explain how to read the basic parts of a financial statement. It will not train you to be an accountant (just as a CPR course will not make you a cardiac doctor), but it should give you the confidence to be able to look at a set of financial statements and make sense of them.**"
>
> From the U.S. Security and Exchange Commission (SEC) *Beginners' Guide to Financial Statement.*
> "

Figure 1. Big 3 Financial Statements

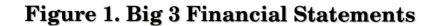

Balance Sheet
... represented by slices of an apple pie

Income Statement
... represented by a stack of Oreo® Cookies

Cash Flow Statement
... represented by a stack of quarters

Introduction *(What is on the menu.)*

Financial statements are simply summaries and structured presentations of the various events (business transactions) that affect a company's financial performance. The owners of the company (shareholders), creditors, and the government (think IRS) are very interested in this stuff

Business transactions are anything that transfers money to or from the company, or transfers goods and services to or from the company. Transactions can also record future financial obligations that the company may assume, or also rights that the company is granted from others. (More on these rights and obligations later.)

The Big 3 Statements

Three numeric presentations document a company's financial performance and financial strength. Why three statements? Well, each paints a different, essential picture—the "three-legged stool of company reporting.

- The *Income Statement* shows the manufacturing (or service offerings) and selling actions of the company that result in profit or loss during a period of time (called the "period"). The Income Statement gives a very important perspective on the company's performance — its profitability.

- The *Cash Flow Statement* details the movements of cash into and out of the company for the period. You need money to make money. Running out of cash is bad. Duh.

- The *Balance Sheet* records at the end of a period, what the company owns and what it owes, including the owners' stake called *shareholders' equity*.

I will describe each statement separately (with pictures) and then show how they interact. It will be fun!

Not Rocket Science

This financial reporting stuff is not rocket science. You have learned all the math required to master financial statements by the end of the fourth grade—mostly addition and subtraction. You will need to learn and use the specialized vocabulary, which can be confusing. You will also need to understand the structure and appreciate the purpose of the three major numeric statements that describe a company's financial condition.

Here is a hint. Watch where money, goods, and services flow. Summarizing and documenting the movements of cash and product is all that financial statements do. It is no more complicated than that. Everything else is details (and some Sanskrit that you do not really need).

People go to college to learn accounting and spend years of apprenticeship figuring out how to use the rules. However, for us regular folks, an overview and general appreciation is easy, possible, and important for everyone in business to know. Read on.

Vocabulary is Important

The purpose of financial statements is to communicate financial information in a way that everyone can understand. Thus, vocabulary is important. As with any specialized field of study, accounting and financial reporting has a language all its own. Unfortunately, some accounting words mean different things than in common parlance. Even within

---

Financial statements document the movement of cash and goods and services into and out of the enterprise. That is all financial statements are about. It is no more complicated. Everything else is details. Don't sweat the details.

the profession, different words can be used to mean the same thing. Aargh!

Just a few examples to chew on...

1. *Sales, shipments,* and *revenue* all mean the same thing.
2. *Profits, earnings,* and *income* all mean the same things.
3. Thus, *revenue* and *income* **do not** mean the same thing! ("Top line" vs. "bottom line.")
4. *Profits* on the Income Statement are different from *cash* on the Balance Sheet.
5. *Orders* are not *sales* until they are shipped to customers.

Got all this? I do not expect you to understand just yet. However, after reading the rest of this short book, you will find enlightenment! I promise.

> **The glossary at the end of this book contains useful definitions and explanations of accounting terms and structures. Take a look!**

Play by the rules!

Owners, creditors, and the government have a significant financial interest in the company's business performance. All three want accurate and timely information in a format that they can understand and is comparable to other similar companies. To this end, accountants have written a clear set of reporting rules for a company's management under which to play and communicate results. These rules are applied in an audit, so they are good to know.

Who makes the rules?

FASB makes the rules and they are called GAAP. Accounting alphabet soup! Sigh.

The Financial Accounting Standards Board (*FASB*) is a private, nonprofit organization made up of Certified Public Accountants (*CPAs*) whose purpose is to develop generally accepted accounting principles (*GAAP*), the standards of financial accounting and reporting used for guidance and education of the public, issuers, auditors, and other users of financial information.

The Olden Days

Back in the olden days when systematic accounting and statement presentation was first developed, the monks would first write down each and every transaction chronologically in a series of other separate books called *Journals,* each containing similar transaction types (called *accounts*). The transactions were then transferred to a book called the *General Ledger* where transactions were grouped by specific accounts. Debits are added to asset accounts and subtracted from liability accounts. *Credits* are subtracted from asset accounts and added to liability accounts.

Literally, "the books" of a company were just that, the company's financial records!

At the end of a period of time (the accounting period), the monks would add up the values of all like transactions recorded in the general ledger and present the totals on separate lines in the statement summaries.

Thus, double entry bookkeeping was born. Now with computers, we just code each transaction with the amount, date, and type and put it in a big computer database. Double entry bookkeeping with its passé debits and credits is outdated as are the quill pens that the monks used.

———

We will focus on manufacturing companies. Other types — retailers, distributors, service providers — have similar, but simpler structured financial statements. Product costing and inventory valuation in manufacturing companies adds complexity to the statements. If you can understand manufacturing accounting, then the other company types are easy.

Credit: Leo Cullum / The New Yorker Collection / The Cartoon Bank
Used with permission.

Figure 2. Income Statement Components:
Sales, Costs, Expenses, Tax, & Income

SALES

COST OF GOODS SOLD (COGS)

Inventory Value of Product
Shipped in the Period

SG&A EXPENSES

Sales, General, & Administrative
Expenses in the Period

GROSS MARGIN

TAX

INCOME *AFTER TAX*

also called Profit After Tax
or PAT

INCOME *PRE-TAX*

Chapter 1. Income Statement

The company's *Income Statement* reports its sales, costs, expenses and profits (or losses) for a period of time — a month, a quarter, or a year. All the company's sales are grouped and presented as a single line item. Another line presents the inventory values of what was sold (*cost of goods sold*).

Another name for the Income Statement is the *Profit & Loss Statement*, or P&L for short.

> — Income Statement —
> **What comes in (sales), what goes out (costs and expenses), and what stays (income).**

On the facing page, **Figure 2** shows this relationship graphically. The standard tabular version of this statement is shown at the end of this chapter.

There are four major elements in the Income Statement presentation: sales, costs, expenses, and income. We will discuss each in order, top to bottom on the Income Statement. Having cookies on hand will help your understanding.

- **Sales** are recorded on the Income Statement when the company actually ships products to the customer. Just receiving an order is not considered a sale.

  Revenue, shipments, or the so-called "top line" are other words that mean the same as "sales."

- **Costs** on the Income Statement are the dollar values of the inventory shipped and recorded as sales. Costs are often called cost-of-goods sold—the inventory value of what was sold.

Reported sales and inventory value are always matched on the statement for the period. Sales and their associated cost-of-goods need to be recorded in the same period to correctly compute profits for the period.

As shown graphically on the next page in **Figure 2**, costs-of-goods (and the value of inventory shipped) is made up of three elements:

1. **Materials**, cost of the purchased raw materials in the product sold and shipped,
2. **Labor**, cost of payroll (including benefits) of people who produce product,
3. **Manufacturing Overhead**, the general costs associated with facilities (rent, heat, light, and power, machinery use) and labor supervision that are attributed to the product sold — a catchall.

Inventory can be valued in two different ways, depending on when the particular widget was manufactured and placed into the company's inventory:

1. **FIFO**, meaning "first-in; first-out," or
2. **LIFO**, meaning "last-in; first-out."

Identical widgets made at different times, can have different inventory values because of inflation, variation in labor required, or perhaps different costs of purchased materials. Either method of inventory valuation is acceptable under GAAP, but a company must choose one method or the other and use it consistently.

FIFO is a more conservative method since income is generally lower. See LIFO and FIFO definitions in the glossary for a more detailed discussion of inventory valuation.

> ## INCOME STATEMENT EQUATION
> ## Sales − Costs − Expenses − Tax = Income
> *...for the period*

Figure 3. Cost & Expense Components

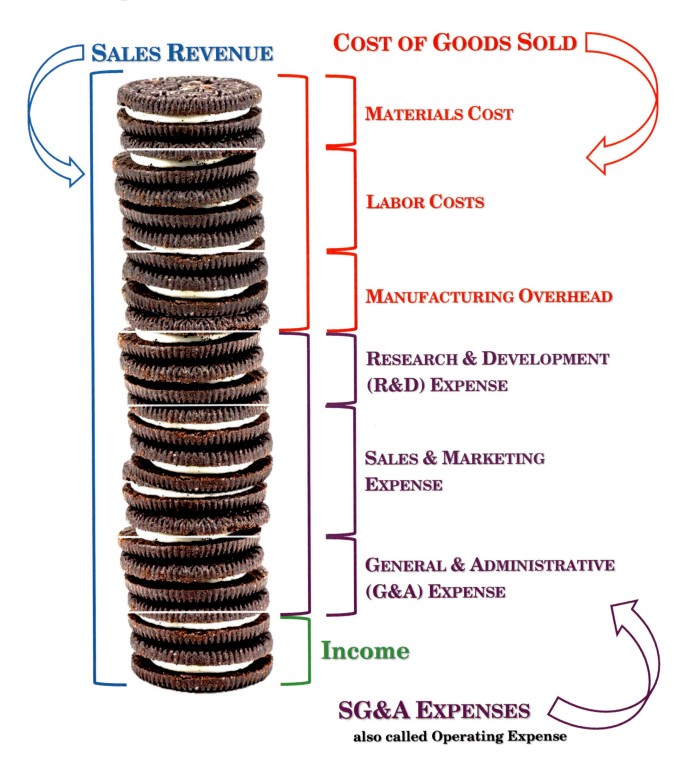

- **Expenses** Operating expenses (also called SG&A, short for selling, general, and administrative expenses) pay for those actions that the company performs during the period to generate operating income.

  Expenses here on the Income Statement are different from "expenditures" as shown on the Cash Flow Statement (more later in **Chapter 4**). Expenditures cash outlays. Expenses are obligations to pay that show up on the Balance sheet as accounts payable (more later in **Chapter 2**). Definitely need a cookie break here!

- **Income** If sales exceed the costs plus expenses, then the business has earned income. If costs plus expenses exceeds sales, then a loss has occurred for the period. Oops.

  Earnings, profits (losses), or the "bottom-line" mean the same as income. Income comes in two flavors, pre-tax (PBT or EBT for "earnings before tax") and after-tax (PAT). Yum. See **Figure 2.**

  Companies can also generate income from finance-only transactions such as receiving interest or by making a profit when selling an asset such as a building. Non-operating income is reported on different statement lines.

Complete Financial Picture?

Each of the three major financial statements views the company's financial health from a different — and very important — perspective. Each statement is related to the others in specific ways. There are natural connections among the statements. More in **Chapter 4**. More cookies now?

The Income Statement gives one very important perspective on the financial health of the business—its profitability. However, the Income Statement does not tell the whole picture. It is just one leg of the 3-legged stool.

The Balance Sheet (**Chapter 2**) reports on assets, liabilities, and equity. The Cash Flow Statement (**Chapter 3**) reports on the cash movements into and out of the company.

Figure 4 below shows the standard tabular presentation of the Income Statement seen in financial reports. Companies do not normally report results using stacks of Oreo® cookies. Their loss.

Figure 4. Income Statement in Tabular Format
...for the period

SALES	Ⓐ
COST OF GOODS SOLD	Ⓑ
GROSS MARGIN	Ⓐ–Ⓑ=Ⓒ
RESEARCH & DEVELOPMENT	Ⓓ
SALES & MARKETING	Ⓔ
GENERAL & ADMINISTRATIVE	Ⓕ
OPERATING EXPENSES	Ⓓ+Ⓔ+Ⓕ=Ⓖ
INCOME FROM OPERATIONS	Ⓒ–Ⓖ=Ⓗ
INTEREST INCOME (EXPENSE)	Ⓘ
INCOME TAXES	Ⓙ
NET INCOME	Ⓗ+Ⓘ–Ⓙ=Ⓚ

Figure 5. Balance Sheet Components:
Assets, Liabilities, & Shareholders' Equity

ASSETS

LIABILITIES

SHAREHOLDERS'
EQUITY

Analogous to "Net Worth"
of an individual person.

Chapter 2. Balance Sheet

It is called the *Balance Sheet* because this financial statement is always "in balance." A company's assets equals its liabilities plus its shareholders' equity. A simpler way to state the Balance Sheet equation is: what a company has (its assets) equals what it owes (its liabilities) plus what it is worth (shareholders' equity). In contrast to the Income Statement, which sums transactions over a period of time, the Balance Sheet is written for a specific date, normally the last day of an accounting period, a month, quarter, or year.

Total Assets   Total Liabilities & Shareholders' Equity

> ### — Balance Sheet —
> ### What the company has,
> ### what the company owes, and
> ### what the shareholders own.

On the facing page, **Figure 5** shows this relationship graphically. The standard tabular version of this statement is shown at the end of the chapter.

Accounting Basis

The *basis of accounting* refers to the methodology under which revenues and expenses are recognized in the financial statements of a company. GAAP recognizes two: cash basis and accrual basis.

Cash Basis of Accounting

In cash basis accounting—used in small businesses and many service companies—all expenses are recorded in the Income Statement when they are paid for in cash, without regard for when goods or services were provided or billed by the seller. Cash books look just like a personal bank statement or check register with chronological entries.

Accrual Basis of Accounting

Almost all large companies—and all those with inventory—use the accrual basis of accounting. Expenses are recorded on the Income Statement in the period in which the company incurs the *obligation to pay*, not when cash actually changes hands.

In accrual accounting, sales are recorded when products are shipped, but before payment is received. The asset, *accounts receivable,* shows these to-be-in-the-future payments.

Similarly, in accrual accounting, expenses are recorded when they are incurred, not when paid. Yet unpaid expenses are recorded as a liability on the Balance Sheet as *accounts payable* or as an *accrued expense.*

Accrual accounting reflects the ebb and flow of business decisions and activities, not just cash flow. In addition, accrual basis accounting best assigns profits to a particular period, of great interest to the I.R.S.

We will discuss accrual basis accounting in the rest of this book. If you understand accrual basis, then cash basis is easy!

> ## BALANCE SHEET EQUATION
> ## Assets = Liabilities + Shareholders' Equity
> ## *...at the end of a period*

Figure 6. Balance Sheet: Assets

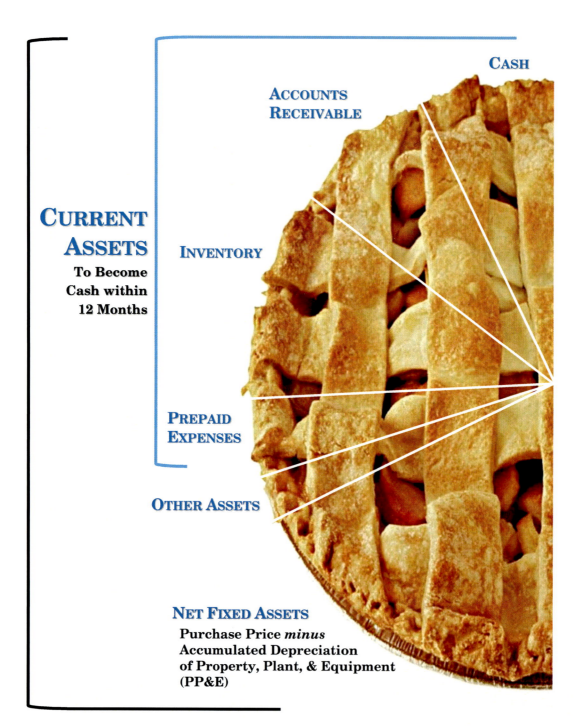

CASH

ACCOUNTS
RECEIVABLE

CURRENT
ASSETS
To Become
Cash within
12 Months

INVENTORY

PREPAID
EXPENSES

OTHER ASSETS

NET FIXED ASSETS
Purchase Price *minus*
Accumulated Depreciation
of Property, Plant, & Equipment
(PP&E)

TOTAL ASSETS

Assets

Assets are everything the company owns: the cash in the bank, inventory, equipment, buildings—all of it. Assets are also certain "rights" owned that have monetary value, such as the right to collect cash from customers who owe the company (accounts receivable).

Asset line items on the Balance Sheet are listed in order of decreasing liquidity (the speed at which they can be turned into cash).

- **Cash** is the ultimate liquid asset and includes on-demand deposits in the bank as well as dollars and cents in the petty cash drawer.

- **Accounts receivable** is money owed to the company from clients (*accounts*) who have received services or goods on credit and who have yet to pay for them.

- **Inventory** are products ready for sale to clients, work-in-process (unfinished products still being manufactured), and any raw materials on-hand for making into products later.

    Inventory values will be used to calculate cost of goods sold on the Income State-
ment when products are sold and shipped to customers.

- **Prepaid expenses** are bills the company has paid, with cash, for services the company has yet to receive.

The above four asset categories make up the company's *Current Assets*. These assets are expected to be turned into cash for company use within the next 12 months.

- **Other Assets** is a catch-all including intangible assets such as goodwill, value of patents, and such. See the Glossary.

- **Net Fixed Assets** (PP&E: property, plant & equipment) is valued at historical cost (purchase price) less an annual charge to the Income Statement called *depreciation* that attempts to account for loss in value of the asset over time. See the Glossary.

    Net means all the prior years' historical costs minus the sum of all depreciation charges (accumulated depreciation).

Figure 7 below shows the Assets section of the Balance Sheet. Don't eat the apple pie just yet. Liabilities to follow.

Figure 7. Balance Sheet Tabular Format

...at period end

—— **Assets** ——————————————

CASH	ⓐ
ACCOUNTS RECEIVABLE	ⓑ
INVENTORY	ⓒ
PREPAID EXPENSE	ⓓ
CURRENT ASSETS	ⓐ+ⓑ+ⓒ+ⓓ=ⓔ
OTHER ASSETS	ⓕ
FIXED ASSETS @ COST	ⓖ
ACCUMULATED DEPRECIATION	ⓗ
NET FIXED ASSETS	ⓖ+ⓗ=ⓘ
TOTAL ASSETS	ⓔ+ⓕ+ⓘ=ⓙ

Figure 8. Balance Sheet: Liabilities & Equity

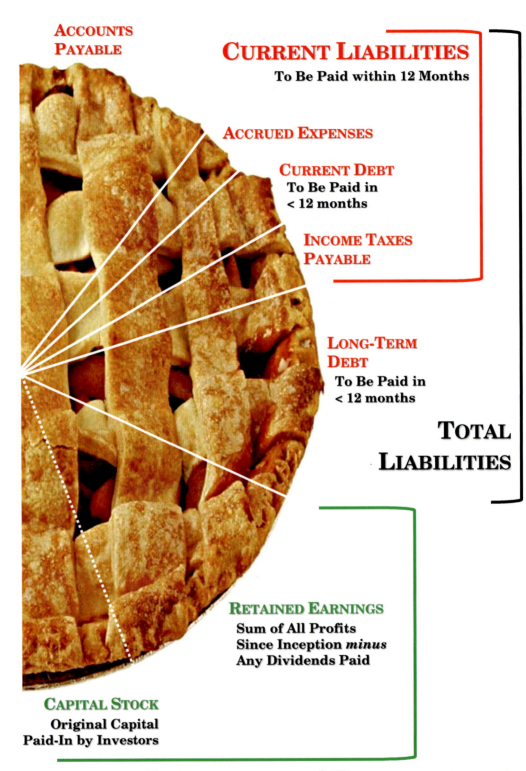

ACCOUNTS PAYABLE

CURRENT LIABILITIES
To Be Paid within 12 Months

ACCRUED EXPENSES

CURRENT DEBT
To Be Paid in
< 12 months

INCOME TAXES PAYABLE

LONG-TERM DEBT
To Be Paid in
< 12 months

TOTAL LIABILITIES

RETAINED EARNINGS
Sum of All Profits
Since Inception *minus*
Any Dividends Paid

CAPITAL STOCK
Original Capital
Paid-In by Investors

SHAREHOLDERS' EQUITY

Liabilities

Liabilities are economic obligations of the company. Pay before eating all the cookies.

- **Accounts Payable** are the amounts owed to suppliers for supplies and materials bought on credit by the company as well as services rendered to the company that are invoiced, but not yet paid.

- **Accrued Expenses** are amounts due to suppliers and service providers for goods and services the company has received and is obligated to pay for, but for which no invoices has been received. Once an invoice is received, the charges become accounts *payable.*

- **Current Debt** is money owed to banks or other creditors that is to be repaid in less than 12 months.

- **Income Taxes Payable** are taxes due, but not yet paid to the government.

The above four liability categories are included in the company's *Current Liabilities,* that is, what the company expects to pay with cash in the next 12 months. The company's *Current Assets* will provide this cash.

- **Long-Term Debt** is the money owed to banks or to other creditors that is planned to be repaid in more than one year.

Shareholders' Equity

Shareholders' equity is a special "liability" of the company signifying an obligation to the company's owners, its shareholders. The shareholders "own" the value of shareholders' equity. Shareholders' equity is also called the company's *net worth.*

- **Capital Stock** is the original money that shareholders paid the company when purchasing shares of stock, *plus*

- **Retained Earnings** are all the earnings that the company has made since formation minus any dividends paid to shareholders by the company over time. Dividends paid to shareholders lowers the value of retained earnings.

Figure 9. Balance Sheet Tabular Format
...at period end

———Liabilities & Shareholders' Equity ———

ACCOUNTS PAYABLE	ⓚ
ACCRUED EXPENSES	ⓛ
CURRENT PORTION OF DEBT	ⓜ
INCOME TAXES PAYABLE	ⓝ
CURRENT LIABILITIES	ⓚ+ⓛ+ⓜ+ⓝ=ⓞ
LONG-TERM DEBT	ⓟ
CAPITAL STOCK	ⓠ
RETAINED EARNINGS	ⓡ
SHAREHOLDERS' EQUITY	ⓠ+ⓡ=ⓢ
TOTAL LIABILITIES & EQUITY	ⓞ+ⓟ+ⓢ=ⓣ

Figure 10. Cash Flow Statement
Cash In & Out

BEGINNING CASH

+ CASH IN

Cash Receipts.
Net Borrowings, and
Sale of Stock

= ENDING CASH

— CASH OUT

Cash Disbursements,
Fixed Asset Purchases, and
Income Taxes Paid

Chapter 3. Cash Flow Statement

Think of the company's *Cash Flow Statement* as a bank statement, reporting all the company's payments (cash disbursements) and deposits (cash receipts) for a period of time. If no actual cash changes hands in a particular transaction, (for example, selling a product on credit, receiving supplies from a vendor, recording depreciation charges, and so forth), the Cash Flow Statement is not changed. However, the Balance Sheet and the Income Statement may be modified by these so-called "non-cash transactions."

Cash comes into a company when the customer pays for the product, not when the company ships it. Cash moves out of the company when it pays for materials, not when the company orders or receives them. Paying salaries lowers cash; paying for equipment lowers cash; paying off a loan lowers cash. Receiving money increases cash, selling stock raises cash; receiving money from customers raises cash too.

A **positive cash flow** for a period means the company has more cash at the end of the period than at the beginning. A **negative cash flow** for a period means the company has less cash at the end of the period than at the beginning. The company could still be profitable, but it is just using more cash than it is bring in. This state of events is common in rapidly growing companies that need a constant infusion of cash borrowings or stock sales to supply needed cash to support that growth.

———

On the facing page, **Figure 10** shows this relationship graphically. The standard tabular version of this statement is shown on the page 18. Here are the definitions of each line item on the statement:

Beginning Cash Balance is the amount of cash the company has on hand at the beginning of the period.

- **Cash Receipts** (also called collections) comes from collecting money from customers. Cash receipts increase the amount of cash the company has on hand as shown on the Balance Sheet.

  Cash receipts are not profits. Profits are something else altogether. Do not confuse the two or no more cookies for you. Profits are reported on the Income Statement.

- **Cash Disbursements** (also called payments) are writing a check to pay for rent, for inventory and supplies or for workers' wages. Cash disbursements lower the amount of cash the company has on hand as shown on the Balance Sheet.

  Cash disbursements as payments to suppliers lower the amount the company owes as reported as accounts payable on the Balance Sheet.

Cash from Operations (Cash Receipts minus Cash Disbursements) reports the flow of money into and out of the business from making and selling products or services. Cash from Operations is the most important ongoing element of cash flow.

Other major cash flows are buying fixed assets, selling stock or making loan payments.

- **Fixed Asset Purchases** include money spent to buy property, plant, and equipment (PP&E) as an investment in the long-term capability of the company to

---

CASH FLOW STATEMENT EQUATION
Start Cash + Cash In − Cash Out = End Cash
...for the period

manufacture and sell products or provides services.

When a company records depreciation charges in the Income Statement, no cash is used and no check is written. The only cash used was when the company originally paid for the equipment purchased.

- **Net Borrowings.** Borrowing money increases the amount of cash the company has on hand. Conversely, paying back a loan decreases cash. The difference between any new borrowings and the amount paid back in the period is called *net borrowings.*

- **Income Taxes Paid.** *Owing* income taxes is different from actually *paying* them. The business owes more income tax every time it sells something for a profit.

  However, just owing taxes does not reduce cash. Only writing a check to the government, and thus paying the taxes due, lowers cash.

- **Sale of Stock.** When people invest in a company's stock, they exchange one piece of paper for another: real U.S. currency for a fancy stock certificate.

When a company sells stock to new investors (now shareholders), it receives money that increases its cash.

- **Ending Cash Balance.** The beginning cash balance (at the start of the period) plus or minus all cash transactions that took place during the period, equals the ending cash balance.

Bankrupt!

If a company has a continuing negative cash flow, it runs the risk of running out of the cash needed to pay its bills when they become due. Just another way of saying broke, tapped-out, insolvent. Creditors can sue for payment and drive the company into bankruptcy. Companies can sustain long stretches without profits, but running out of cash is different. With no gas in the tank, everything just stops. Companies fail this way. Sigh.

———

In the next chapter, we will show how the three major financial statements interact in showing the true financial picture of the company. Time for the cookie eating frenzy to begin.

Figure 11. Cash Flow Statement Tabular Format
...*for the period*

BEGINNING CASH BALANCE	①
CASH RECEIPTS	②
CASH DISBURSEMENTS	③
CASH FROM OPERATIONS	②−③=④
FIXED ASSET PURCHASES	⑤
NET BORROWINGS	⑥
INCOME TAXES PAID	⑦
SALES OF STOCK	⑧
ENDING CASH BALANCE	①+④−⑤+⑥−⑦+⑧=⑨

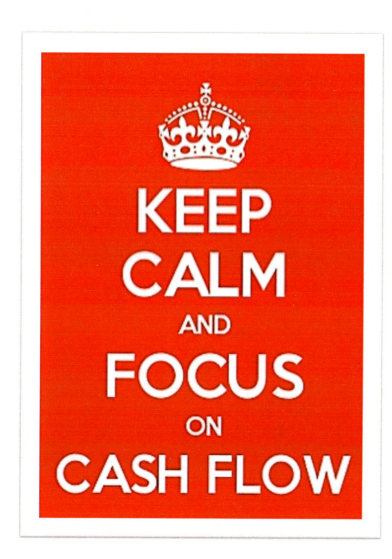

Figure 12. Balance Sheet Connections

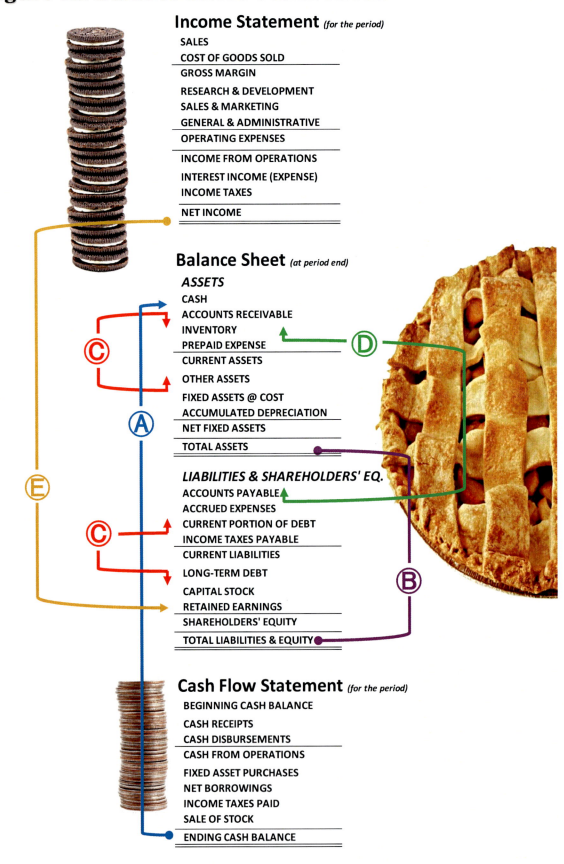

Income Statement *(for the period)*

SALES

COST OF GOODS SOLD

GROSS MARGIN

RESEARCH & DEVELOPMENT

SALES & MARKETING

GENERAL & ADMINISTRATIVE

OPERATING EXPENSES

INCOME FROM OPERATIONS

INTEREST INCOME (EXPENSE)

INCOME TAXES

NET INCOME

Balance Sheet *(at period end)*

ASSETS

CASH

ACCOUNTS RECEIVABLE

INVENTORY

PREPAID EXPENSE

CURRENT ASSETS

OTHER ASSETS

FIXED ASSETS @ COST

ACCUMULATED DEPRECIATION

NET FIXED ASSETS

TOTAL ASSETS

LIABILITIES & SHAREHOLDERS' EQ.

ACCOUNTS PAYABLE

ACCRUED EXPENSES

CURRENT PORTION OF DEBT

INCOME TAXES PAYABLE

CURRENT LIABILITIES

LONG-TERM DEBT

CAPITAL STOCK

RETAINED EARNINGS

SHAREHOLDERS' EQUITY

TOTAL LIABILITIES & EQUITY

Cash Flow Statement *(for the period)*

BEGINNING CASH BALANCE

CASH RECEIPTS

CASH DISBURSEMENTS

CASH FROM OPERATIONS

FIXED ASSET PURCHASES

NET BORROWINGS

INCOME TAXES PAID

SALE OF STOCK

ENDING CASH BALANCE

Chapter 4. Entering Transactions

The three major financial statements — *Income Statement, Balance Sheet and Cash Flow Statement* — are all connected. Transactions that make changes in one statement often necessitate changes in another.

In this chapter, we will describe the cascade of financial statement entries that record basic company transactions including the:

- **Sales Cycle** How sales and payment transactions are recorded on all three financial statements. See **Figure 13**.

- **Expense Cycle** How expense and expenditure transactions are recorded on all three statements as well. See **Figure 14.**

- **Investment Cycle** How equity sales and debt transactions are recorded on the *Balance Sheet* and *Cash Flow Statement*. The *Income Statement* is not affected. See **Figure 15**.

- **Fixed Asset & Depreciation** How property, plant, and equipment (PP&E) purchase transactions are recorded on the *Balance Sheet* and *Cash Flow Statement.* Depreciation transactions modify the *Income Statement* and the *Balance Sheet* but not the *Cash Flow Statement.* See **Figure 16**.

————

The *Income Statement* describes the sales transactions that result in income or loss. The *Cash Flow Statement* describes the flow of cash into and out of the company. The *Balance Sheet* ties these two statements together. This chapter describes these connections.

Further, the Balance Sheet structure requires that assets always equals liabilities and shareholders' equity. Sort of keeping the *Income Statement* and *Cash Flow Statement* honest. Everything must add up!

Balance Sheet Connections

(A) **Ending Cash Balance** on the *Cash Flow Statement* for the period always equals **Cash** at period end on the *Balance Sheet*.

(B) As per the basic equation of accounting (see page 9), **Total Assets** always equals **Total Liabilities & Shareholders'** Equity on the *Balance Sheet*.

(C) To keep the *Balance Sheet* in balance, when a transaction amount is added (or subtracted) to an asset account, an equal amount must be subtracted (or added) from another asset account. Likewise for liability accounts. In both cases, **Total Assets** or **Total Liabilities & Shareholders' Equity** do not change and maintains the balance in the Balance sheet. Got that?

(D) Also, the *Balance Sheet* remains in balance if an equal amount is added (or subtracted) from an asset account and a liability account. Thus, **Total Assets** or **Total Liabilities & Shareholders' Equity** increase (or decrease) by the same amount to maintain the balance in the *Balance Sheet*. Have a cookie.

(E) An increase in **Net Income** on the *Income Statement* is added to **Retained Earnings** on the *Balance Sheet*. A loss would be subtracted to both accounts. Thus, **Total Assets** or **Total Liabilities & Shareholders' Equity** increase (or decrease) by the same amount to maintain the balance in the *Balance Sheet*.

Figure 13. The Sales Cycle
Recording sales and payments.

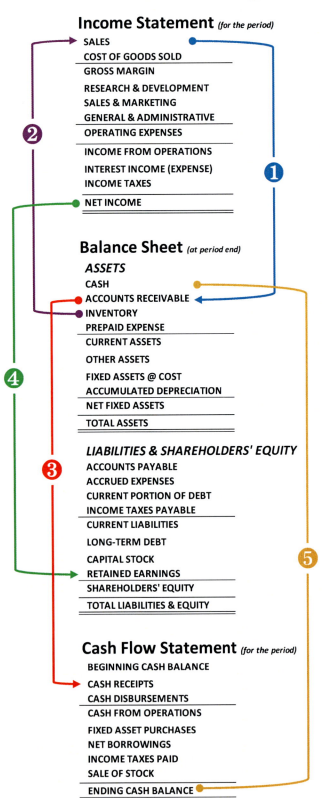

Sales Cycle Connections

1 When a sales is made on credit, **Sales** increases at the top of the *Income Statement* and **Accounts Receivable** increases on the *Balance Sheet* by the same amount.

2 When a sales is made, product value is moved from **Inventory** on the *Balance Sheet* to **Cost of Goods Sold (COGS)** on the *Income Statement.*

3 When the customer pays for the products shipped, the **Accounts Receivable** on the *Balance Sheet* becomes a **Cash Receipt** on the *Cash Flow Statement.*

4 When a sale is entered on the *Income Statement,* **Net Income (Loss)** is generated and is added to **Retained Earnings** on the *Balance Sheet.*

5 **Ending Cash Balance** is increased by the amount added as a **Cash Receipt** in ❸ and equals **Cash** on the *Balance Sheet.*

Balance Sheet Summary

Total Assets on the *Balance Sheet* increase by the **Cash** added in ❺ and decrease by the **Inventory** shipped in ❷. **Accounts Receivable** does not change because the same amount was added in ❶ and then subtracted in ❸.

Total Liabilities & Shareholders' Equity increases by the **Net Income** added to **Retained Earnings** in ❹. This amount is the same as the increase in **Total Assets** as computed in the prior paragraph.

Thus, the *Balance Sheet* remains in balance. *Hallelujah!*

Figure 14. The Expense Cycle
Recording expenses and expenditures.

Expense Cycle Connections

① **Expenses** when incurred are entered on the *Income Statement* and become **Accounts Payable** on the *Balance Sheet.*

② Expenses reduce **Net Income** on the *Income Statement* and also reduce **Retained Earnings** on the *Balance Sheet.*

③ When paid, **Accounts Payable** on the *Balance Sheet* become **Cash Disbursements** and lowers the **Ending Cash Balance** on the *Cash Flow Statements* and also **Cash** on the *Balance Sheet* all by the same amount.

Balance Sheet Summary

In summary, **Total Assets** on the *Balance Sheet* decrease by the amount of **Cash** disbursed in **③**. **Accounts Receivable** does not change because the same amount was added in **①** and then subtracted in **③**.

Total Liabilities & Shareholders' Equity decrease in **②** by the lowered **Net Income** that is also subtracted from **Retained Earnings**. This amount is the same as the decrease in **Total Assets** as computed in the prior paragraph.

Thus, the *Balance Sheet* remains in balance. Perhaps a slice of pie now?

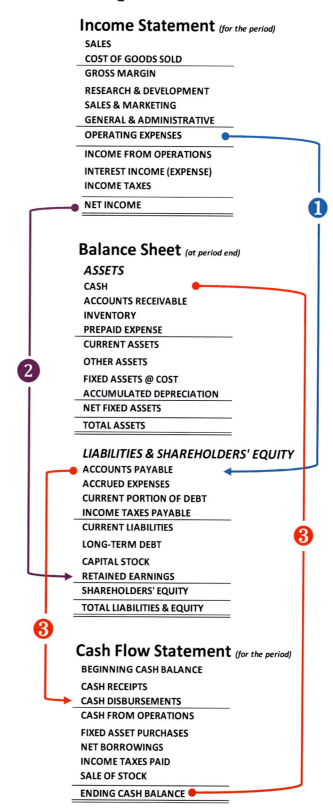

Income Statement *(for the period)*

SALES
COST OF GOODS SOLD
GROSS MARGIN
RESEARCH & DEVELOPMENT
SALES & MARKETING
GENERAL & ADMINISTRATIVE
OPERATING EXPENSES
INCOME FROM OPERATIONS
INTEREST INCOME (EXPENSE)
INCOME TAXES
NET INCOME

Balance Sheet *(at period end)*
ASSETS
CASH
ACCOUNTS RECEIVABLE
INVENTORY
PREPAID EXPENSE
CURRENT ASSETS
OTHER ASSETS
FIXED ASSETS @ COST
ACCUMULATED DEPRECIATION
NET FIXED ASSETS
TOTAL ASSETS

LIABILITIES & SHAREHOLDERS' EQUITY
ACCOUNTS PAYABLE
ACCRUED EXPENSES
CURRENT PORTION OF DEBT
INCOME TAXES PAYABLE
CURRENT LIABILITIES
LONG-TERM DEBT
CAPITAL STOCK
RETAINED EARNINGS
SHAREHOLDERS' EQUITY
TOTAL LIABILITIES & EQUITY

Cash Flow Statement *(for the period)*
BEGINNING CASH BALANCE
CASH RECEIPTS
CASH DISBURSEMENTS
CASH FROM OPERATIONS
FIXED ASSET PURCHASES
NET BORROWINGS
INCOME TAXES PAID
SALE OF STOCK
ENDING CASH BALANCE

Figure 15. The Investment Cycle
Recording equity and debt transactions.

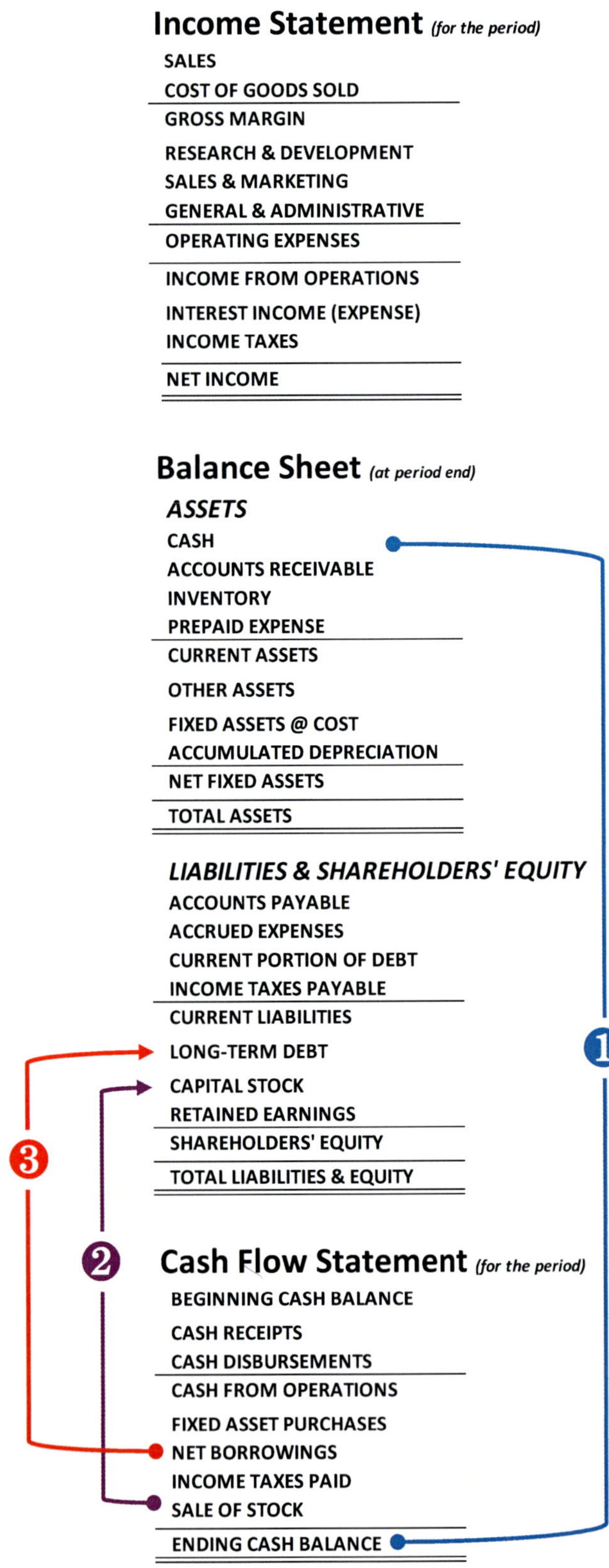

Income Statement *(for the period)*

SALES
COST OF GOODS SOLD
GROSS MARGIN
RESEARCH & DEVELOPMENT
SALES & MARKETING
GENERAL & ADMINISTRATIVE
OPERATING EXPENSES
INCOME FROM OPERATIONS
INTEREST INCOME (EXPENSE)
INCOME TAXES
NET INCOME

Balance Sheet *(at period end)*

ASSETS
CASH
ACCOUNTS RECEIVABLE
INVENTORY
PREPAID EXPENSE
CURRENT ASSETS
OTHER ASSETS
FIXED ASSETS @ COST
ACCUMULATED DEPRECIATION
NET FIXED ASSETS
TOTAL ASSETS

LIABILITIES & SHAREHOLDERS' EQUITY
ACCOUNTS PAYABLE
ACCRUED EXPENSES
CURRENT PORTION OF DEBT
INCOME TAXES PAYABLE
CURRENT LIABILITIES
LONG-TERM DEBT
CAPITAL STOCK
RETAINED EARNINGS
SHAREHOLDERS' EQUITY
TOTAL LIABILITIES & EQUITY

Cash Flow Statement *(for the period)*

BEGINNING CASH BALANCE
CASH RECEIPTS
CASH DISBURSEMENTS
CASH FROM OPERATIONS
FIXED ASSET PURCHASES
NET BORROWINGS
INCOME TAXES PAID
SALE OF STOCK
ENDING CASH BALANCE

Investment Cycle Connections

① Issuing new shares of the company's stock increases **Sale of Stock** and thus **Ending Cash Balance** on the *Cash Flow Statement.*

Ending Cash Balance for the period on the *Cash Flow Statement* must equal **Cash** on the *Balance Sheet* reported at period end.

② **Capital Stock** on the *Balance Sheet* increases by the cash received from the stock sale.

③ **Net Borrowings** when entered on the *Cash Flow Statement* increase both **Cash** and **Debt** on the *Balance Sheet.* Any debt added that must be repaid in less than 12 months would be entered in **Current Portion of Debt**.

Note: Issuing stock or taking on more debt does not affect the *Income Statement.*

Balance Sheet Summary

Total Assets on the *Balance Sheet* increase by the **Cash** added in **②** and **③**.

Total Liabilities & Shareholders' Equity increases by the amount of Capital Stock and the Debt added. This amount is the same as the increase in **Total Assets** as computed in the prior paragraph.

Thus, the *Balance Sheet* remains in balance. Cookies for this effort.

Figure 16. The Fixed Asset Cycle
Recording PP&E transactions and depreciation.

PP&E Connections

① **W**hen equipment (PP&E) is purchased **Fixed Assets at Cost** on the *Balance Sheet* increases by the purchase price.

② **Ending Cash Balance** on the *Cash Flow Statement* is lowered by the purchase price as well as **Cash** is lowered on the *Balance Sheet*.

Since **Cash** is lowered by the amount that **Fixed Assets at Cost** is raised, **Total Assets** does not change, and the *Balance Sheet* remains in balance. ***Hurrah!***

Depreciation Connections

Depreciation is a so-called *non-cash expense*. When a depreciation expense is entered on the *Income Statement* (to account for wear and tear of the equipment) no cash actually leaves the company. Remember, the equipment was previously totally paid for in cash (see above PP&E Connections) when purchased originally.

③ When a depreciation **Operating Expense** is entered in the *Income Statement,* **Accumulated Depreciation** increases by the same amount on the *Balance Sheet.*

④ **Net Income** on the *Income Statement* also decreases by the amount of the expense. **Retained Earnings** are lowered on the *Balance Sheet.*

Since **Accumulated Depreciation** is increased by the same amount that Retained Earnings lowered, **Total Liabilities & Shareholder's Equity** does not change and the *Balance Sheet* remains in balance. ***Hurrah again!***

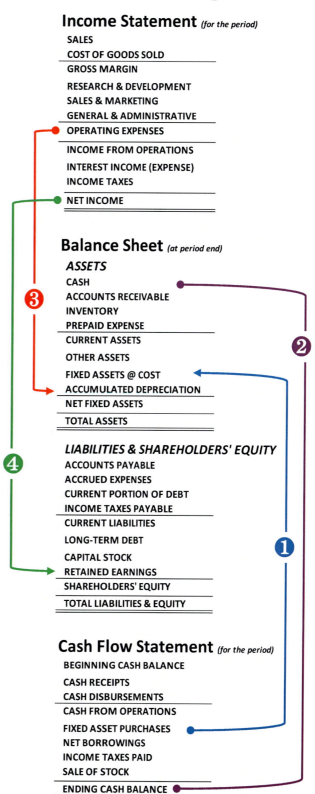

Income Statement *(for the period)*
- SALES
- COST OF GOODS SOLD
- GROSS MARGIN
- RESEARCH & DEVELOPMENT
- SALES & MARKETING
- GENERAL & ADMINISTRATIVE
- OPERATING EXPENSES
- INCOME FROM OPERATIONS
- INTEREST INCOME (EXPENSE)
- INCOME TAXES
- NET INCOME

Balance Sheet *(at period end)*

ASSETS
- CASH
- ACCOUNTS RECEIVABLE
- INVENTORY
- PREPAID EXPENSE
- CURRENT ASSETS
- OTHER ASSETS
- FIXED ASSETS @ COST
- ACCUMULATED DEPRECIATION
- NET FIXED ASSETS
- TOTAL ASSETS

LIABILITIES & SHAREHOLDERS' EQUITY
- ACCOUNTS PAYABLE
- ACCRUED EXPENSES
- CURRENT PORTION OF DEBT
- INCOME TAXES PAYABLE
- CURRENT LIABILITIES
- LONG-TERM DEBT
- CAPITAL STOCK
- RETAINED EARNINGS
- SHAREHOLDERS' EQUITY
- TOTAL LIABILITIES & EQUITY

Cash Flow Statement *(for the period)*
- BEGINNING CASH BALANCE
- CASH RECEIPTS
- CASH DISBURSEMENTS
- CASH FROM OPERATIONS
- FIXED ASSET PURCHASES
- NET BORROWINGS
- INCOME TAXES PAID
- SALE OF STOCK
- ENDING CASH BALANCE

Figure 17. How to Compute Ratios.

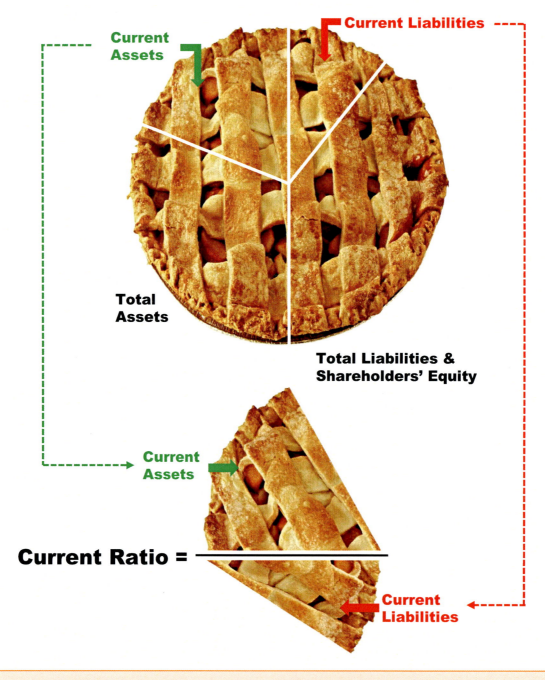

Current Ratio = Current Assets / Current Liabilities

$$\text{Current Ratio} = \frac{\text{Current Assets}}{\text{Current Liabilities}}$$

Chapter 5. Financial Ratios & Analysis

It is not so much the absolute numbers of sales revenue, costs, expenses, assets, and liabilities that are important in judging the financial condition of a company, but rather, the relationship between these numbers. Ratios analysis can focus your efforts to where they will do the most good for your business performance.

Ratio analysis (that is, comparing one number on a company's financial statements with another number) is most useful when you wish to compare:

1. Year-to-year performance to determine if things are getting better or getting worse for the company, or

2. The other companies in an industry to see which is performing best given their common constraints. In which would you rather invest? A company with good performance ratios or a company with poor ones?

3. Where your investing dollar might bring the highest return. Does the growth prospects of the company and the profitability ratios justify such a high stock price?

Companies in different industries can have widely different ratios. Different industries require different capital structures and have different operating characteristics, thus different ratio values.

A supermarket business is financially different from a software development business, which is different from an electric utility, which is different from an automobile manufacturer ... *get the picture?*

———

The circled letters and numbers in the ratio equations represent the tabular format line items as shown for the Income Statement (page 9), Balance Sheet (pages 13 and 15), and Cash Flow Statement (page 18) in this book.

Liquidity Ratio

The liquidity ratio reports on the ability of a company to pay its bills.

1. The **Current Ratio** is the best-known indicator of short-term financial strength. It measures whether current assets (cash and other assets that are expected to be converted into cash within the year) are sufficient to pay current liabilities (those obligations that must be paid within the year). A 1.5 to 1 ratio is considered good.

Industry & Company Comparisons

Just looking at a single ratio does not really tell you much about a company. You also need a standard of comparison, a benchmark. There are three principal benchmarks used in ratio analysis.

History How has the ratio changed over time? Are things getting better or worse for the company? Is gross margin going down, indicating that costs are rising faster than prices can be increased? Are receivable days lengthening, indicating that there are payment problems?

Competition If a company has a significantly higher return on assets than a competitor does, it strongly suggests that the company manages its resources better.

Industry Industry-wide average ratios are collected and published and can give an analyst a good starting point in assessing a particular company's financial performance.

Figure 18 on page 31 shows various ratios of various industries. Note, there can be large difference in ratio values for different industries. Later in this chapter, we will explain why.

———

More useful ratios to compute are shown on the next pages.

Profitability Ratios

Profitability ratios are the common "return on" ratios. These ratios measure management's ability to turn a profit, given a level of resources.

1. **Return on Assets** measures success in employing the company's assets to generate a profit. The higher the better.

$$\text{Return on Assets} = \frac{\text{Net Income } Ⓚ}{\text{Total Assets } Ⓙ}$$

2. **Return on Equity** measures the company's success in maximizing return on the shareholders' investment. Again, the higher the better.

$$\text{Return on Equity} = \frac{\text{Net Income } Ⓚ}{\text{Shareholders' Equity } Ⓢ}$$

3. **Return on Sales**, also sometimes called *profit margin*, compares what is left over (profits, or loss) when all expenses and costs are subtracted from sales.

$$\text{Return on Sales} = \frac{\text{Net Income } Ⓚ}{\text{Sales } Ⓐ}$$

4. **Gross Margin** measures how much it costs the company to make its products and, consequently, how much the company can spend in SG&A expense and still make a profit.

$$\text{Gross Margin} = \frac{\text{Sales } Ⓐ - \text{COGS } Ⓑ}{\text{Sales } Ⓐ}$$

Asset Management Ratios

Asset management ratios show how efficiently and effectively the company uses the financial resources available to it.

1. **Inventory Turn** measures the level of business that can be conducted with a given investment in inventory, the lower the inventory relative to sales, the better.

$$\text{Inventory Turn} = \frac{\text{COGS } \text{Ⓑ}}{\text{Inventory } \text{©}}$$

2. **Asset Turn Ratio** measures the efficiency of asset use. A high asset turn means that the company can expand sales with a low capital investment.

$$\text{Asset Turn} = \frac{\text{Revenue } \text{Ⓐ}}{\text{Total Assets } \text{Ⓙ}}$$

3. **Receivable Days** shows, on average, how long after shipment of product until its payment comes in. The longer the wait in days, the more capital is tied up in customer financing.

$$\text{Receivable Days} = \frac{\text{Receivables } \text{ⓑ} \times 365}{\text{Revenue } \text{Ⓐ}}$$

Leverage Ratios

Leverage ratios measure how much of the company's assets are financed with debt. Leverage is using other people's money (OPM) to generate profits for yourself. By substituting debt for equity dollars (your own money), you can hope to make more profit per your invested dollar.

More ratios follow...

1. **Debt to Equity** shows how much debt the company has relative to its investor equity.

$$\text{Debt to Equity} = \frac{\text{Debt } \textcircled{m} + \textcircled{p}}{\text{Shareholders' Equity } \textcircled{s}}$$

2. **Debt Ratio** measures the amount of debt relative to total assets of the company. The higher the ratio, the higher the operating leverage (and risk) of the company's operations.

$$\text{Debt Ratio} = \frac{\text{Debt } \textcircled{m} + \textcircled{p}}{\text{Total Assets } \textcircled{j}}$$

Ratio Analysis

Review the industry average financial ratio chart on the facing page.

Question: What can the ratios tell us about companies and industries?

Answer: It is often the nature of their business that some companies are more profitable than others are; some need a lot more inventory than others do; some use a lot of debt to finance their operations; some use their assets more efficiently; and so forth.

Software and high technology industries show a high profitability margin. These high margins allow companies to spend a relatively large amount on sales & marketing expense to drive their growth. They also can support high research & development expenses to increase proprietary technology while still being highly profitable.

In contrast, retail companies have low *gross margins*. They are resellers of other company's products and thus their *cost-of goods* is relatively high. *Profit margins* tend to be low in retail industries as well. However, retail has low *accounts receivable days* since they are mostly cash businesses.

The high *debt to equity* ratios for retail stores indicates use of leverage. By carrying debt, these companies can stock their shelves and achieve a normal *return on equity* in a business that offers only a low *return on assets*.

Note, there is not much room for mistakes in businesses with a very low *return on sales*. For supermarkets, only 1¢ on a dollar of sales turns into profit. In contrast, software companies earn much, much more per dollar of sales.

Fresh food related companies such as restaurants and supermarkets have high *inventory turns* because of the perishable nature of their product ingredients. Use it or lose it.

Note that supermarkets and retail have low accounts receivables as measured in *receivable days*. Not surprising, since both industries are so-called "cash businesses" with little credit given to customers.

Figure 18. Financial Ratios by Industry

Industry	Liquidity Ratio	Asset Ratios			Profitability Ratios				Leverage Ratio
	Current Ratio	Inventory Turn	Receivable Days	Asset Turn	Gross Margin	Return on Sales	Return on Asssets	Return on Equity	Debt to Equity
Airlines	1.3	16	23	0.8	59%	3.5%	6.0%	11.6%	1.9
Apparel Manufacturing	2.1	5	85	1.1	41%	1.8%	5.7%	3.0%	0.9
Banking	0.8	n/a	n/a	n/a	n/a	n/a	2.0%	2.1%	6.4
Broadcasting	0.8	12	99	0.4	84%	5.0%	5.7%	9.9%	1.2
Chemicals	1.0	9	91	0.5	19%	1.7%	4.3%	3.4%	1.9
Computer Manufacture	1.0	15	114	0.5	37%	8.2%	7.5%	11.0%	0.6
Construction Equipment	1.5	6	166	0.6	29%	8.9%	10.0%	21.2%	2.0
Financial Services	1.1	n/a	n/a	0.1	40%	7.7%	2.2%	6.9%	2.1
Hospitals & Health Care	1.7	13	58	1.0	n/a	3.8%	8.1%	4.6%	1.1
Hotels	1.0	n/a	36	0.1	87%	9.0%	11.3%	16.2%	2.5
Information Technologies	2.1	6	73	0.5	61%	3.4%	2.3%	4.5%	0.6
Insurance	0.4	n/a	n/a	0.2	41%	3.4%	2.3%	4.5%	0.6
Oil & Gas Exploration	0.8	28	74	0.4	41%	11.8%	9.0%	11.5%	0.6
Pharmaceuticals	1.1	4	152	0.4	48%	11.4%	7.5%	10.5%	0.8
Restaurants	0.8	18	36	0.7	55%	5.4%	8.7%	14.0%	1.0
Retail	0.7	7	15	1.7	25%	7.5%	9.0%	14.1%	0.8
Software	0.5	23	83	0.4	68%	16.9%	12.4%	19.5%	0.4
Supermarkets	1.0	13	14	2.2	28%	1.0%	5.4%	7.5%	0.8
Telecommunication	0.8	4	122	0.3	88%	5.5%	4.6%	4.2%	0.9
Utilities	1.1	15	32	0.6	33%	6.0%	2.9%	1.7%	1.8

Adapted from **Almanac of Business & Industrial Ratios** by Leo Troy.

FAVORABLE	LESS FAVORABLE

Software companies also have a high inventory turn, but mostly because their inventory is inexpensive and very little capital is required to have lots on-hand.

Banks have lots of debt from depositors required by their capital structure and need to finance and leverage their operations. Thus also, their *return on assets* is low.

Investment Price/Earnings Ratio

The stock market rewards companies with good current and expected performance with high "price to earnings" (PE) ratios. PE ratio measures the stock price vs. the underlying profit per share of the company's stock. For investors the PE ratio is a forward-looking estimate with a large component being factored in for expected longer-term profit growth.

Determining what company's PE ratio "should be" is often a matter of art, not necessarily of analysis. However, if earnings are high, return on equity is high, and earnings are growing, investors tend to pay higher prices for a share of stock. Investors will pay less for a company with low earnings and slow growth.

Of the industry segments show in the table above, high PE ratios are found in software, information technologies, health care, and specialized machinery industries. Low PE ratios are found in broadcasting, telecommunications, utilities, and energy. The rest are in the middle.

———

Try your hand at computing the ratios for your own company. See how they compare. Good luck and treat yourself to some cookies or a piece of pie or both!

Balance Sheet

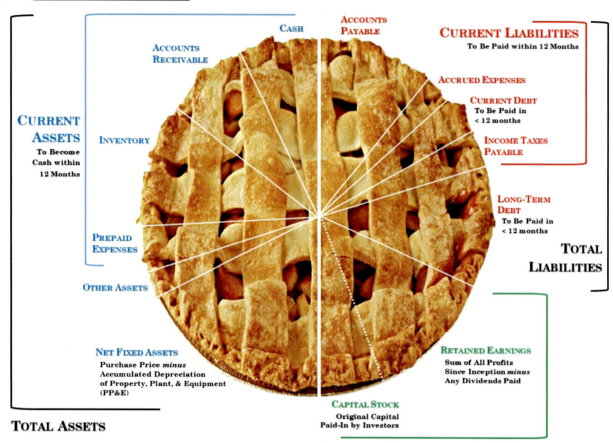

CURRENT ASSETS
To Become Cash within 12 Months

CASH

ACCOUNTS RECEIVABLE

INVENTORY

PREPAID EXPENSES

OTHER ASSETS

NET FIXED ASSETS
Purchase Price *minus* Accumulated Depreciation of Property, Plant, & Equipment (PP&E)

TOTAL ASSETS

ACCOUNTS PAYABLE

CURRENT LIABILITIES
To Be Paid within 12 Months

ACCRUED EXPENSES

CURRENT DEBT
To Be Paid in < 12 months

INCOME TAXES PAYABLE

LONG-TERM DEBT
To Be Paid in < 12 months

TOTAL LIABILITIES

RETAINED EARNINGS
Sum of All Profits Since Inception *minus* Any Dividends Paid

CAPITAL STOCK
Original Capital Paid-In by Investors

SHAREHOLDERS' EQUITY

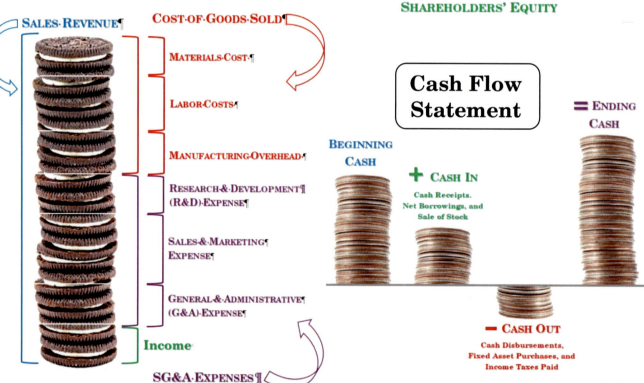

SALES·REVENUE¶

COST·OF·GOODS·SOLD¶

MATERIALS·COST·¶

LABOR·COSTS¶

MANUFACTURING·OVERHEAD·¶

RESEARCH·&·DEVELOPMENT¶ (R&D)·EXPENSE¶

SALES·&·MARKETING¶ EXPENSE¶

GENERAL·&·ADMINISTRATIVE¶ (G&A)·EXPENSE¶

Income·

SG&A·EXPENSES¶
····also-called·Operating·Expense¶

Income Statement

Cash Flow Statement

BEGINNING CASH

+ CASH IN
Cash Receipts, Net Borrowings, and Sale of Stock

= ENDING CASH

– CASH OUT
Cash Disbursements, Fixed Asset Purchases, and Income Taxes Paid

Glossary & Index

ABC

Account

An account is a unique designation for each type of asset, liability, equity, revenue, and expense. Transaction amounts are recorded in accounting ledgers and journals by account. See chart of accounts, ledger, and journal.

Also, a customer. See following definitions.

Accounts payable on the Balance sheet are amounts owed to suppliers for supplies and materials bought on credit as well as services rendered to the company, but for which the invoices are still unpaid.

Accounts receivable on the Balance Sheet is money owed to the company from clients (the *accounts*) who have received services or goods on credit and who have yet to pay for them.

In the accrual basis of accounting, expenses are recorded on the Income Statement in the period in which the company incurs the *obligation to pay*, not when cash actually changes hands.

Accrued Expenses on the Balance Sheet are amounts due to suppliers and service providers for goods and services the company has received and is obligated to pay for, but for which no invoice has been received. Once an invoice is received, the charges become accounts payable.

The sum of all depreciation charges since when a Fixed Asset was purchased

Assets on the Balance Sheet are everything the company owns: the cash in the bank, inventory, equipment, buildings—all of it. Assets are also certain "rights" owned that have monetary value, such as the right to collect cash from customers who owe the company money (accounts receivable).

The accounts management ratio shows how efficiently/effectively the company uses the financial resources available.

See *inventory turn* and *asset turn ratios*.

The asset turn ratio measures the efficiency of asset use. A high asset turn means that the company can expand sales with a low capital investment.

$$Asset\ Turn\ Ratio = \frac{Revenue}{Total\ Assets}$$

The Balance Sheet records what the company owns (assets) and what it owes (liabilities), including the owners stake (shareholders' equity) at the end of the accounting period.

Balance Sheet transactions are those non-cash transactions that only affect the Balance Sheet and not the Income Statement or Cash Flow Statement.

Beginning cash balance in the Cash Flow Statement is the amount of cash the company has on hand at the start of an accounting period.

"Books, The"

"The books" is slang for the accounting and financial records of a company. In the olden days, these records were written down, literally, in books (see *journals* and *ledgers)*.

See Income.

The ups and downs of the economy. Can have a great effect on financial ratio values.

Capital Stock on the Balance Sheet is the original amount of money shareholders paid into the company for purchasing shares of stock.

Cash on the Balance Sheet is the ultimate liquid asset and includes on-demand deposits in the bank as well as dollars and cents in the petty cash drawer.

In cash basis accounting, all expenses are recorded on the Income Statement when they are paid for in cash, irrespective of when goods or services were billed by the seller.

Cash disbursements are cash spent by the company used to pay its bills as shown on the Cash Flow Statement, also called "payments."

The Cash Flow Statement details the movements of cash into and out of the company for an accounting period.

Cash from operations on the Income Statement is revenue (sales) minus SG&A expenses.

Cash receipts, as shown on the Cash Flow Statement, records cash payments from customers. Also called collections or simply receipts.

Chart of Accounts
A chart of accounts (COA) is a financial organizational tool that provides a complete listing of every account in an accounting system. An account is a unique record for each type of asset, liability, equity, revenue, and expense.

Costs
See Cost of Goods Sold.

Cost of Goods Sold on the Income Statement is the dollar value of the inventory shipped and recorded as sales. Reported sales and inventory value are always "matched" on the statement for the period. Sales and their associated cost-of-goods need to be recorded in the same period to correctly compute profits for the period.

Credits are amounts added to asset accounts thus making them bigger. Also, credits mean amounts subtracted from liability accounts making them less small.

Current Assets are Cash, Accounts Payable, Inventory, and Prepaid Expenses—those assets are expected to be turned into cash for company use within the next 12 months. This cash will be used to pay the company's Current Liabilities.

Current Debt is that money owed to banks or other creditors that is to be repaid in less than 12 months.

Current Liabilities are Accounts Payable, Accrued Expenses, Current Debt, and income Taxes Payable—those liabilities for which the company expects to pay with cash in the next 12 months. This cash will be supplied by the company's Current Assets.

The Current Ratio is the most important measure of short-term liquidity and financial strength. Measures whether current assets (cash and other assets that are expected to be converted into cash within the year) are sufficient to pay current liabilities (those obligations that must be paid within the year).

$$Current\ Ratio = \frac{Current\ Assets}{Current\ Liabilities}$$

DEF

Debits are amounts subtracted from asset accounts thus making them smaller. Also, debits mean amounts added to liability accounts making them bigger.

Long-term debt is money owed to banks or other creditors that is to be repaid in more than a year.

Short-term debt is money owed to banks or other creditors that is to be repaid in less than 12 months.

The debt-to-equity ratio shows how much debt the company has relative to its investor equity.

$$Debt\ to\ Equity\ Ratio = \frac{Total\ Debt}{Shareholders'Equity}$$

The debt ratio measures the amount of debt relative to total assets of the company, an indication of leveraged capital structure.

$$Debt\ Ratio = \frac{Total\ Debt}{Total\ Assets}$$

Depreciation is an expense recorded on the Income Statement that attempts to account for loss in value of a fixed asset over time. Net Fixed Assets equals Fixed Assets at Cost minus Accumulated Depreciation.

Disbursements
See Cash Disbursements.

Double entry bookkeeping was developed by monks in the Middle Ages to record and track financial transactions at the monastery. Double entry bookkeeping with its debits and credits is outdated as are the quill pens that the monks used. We use computers now.

Ending cash balance is the amount of cash the company has on hand at the end of an accounting period as shown as cash on the Balance Sheet.

A stock or any other security representing an ownership interest.

Expenditures are the actual spending of money as shown on the Cash Flow Statement. Also called, payments or cash disbursements.

It is important to differentiate "expense" on the Income Statement from "expenditures" An expenditure is made when the company actually pays as a cash disbursement shown on the Cash Flow Statement.

Expenses (also called "operating expenses" or SG&A, for selling, general and administrative) record those actions listed on the Income Statement that the company makes during the period to generate operating income.

Differentiating an "expense" from "an expenditure" is important. In accrual accounting, expenses are recorded when the company commits to pay an expense becoming an accounts payable on the Balance Sheet, not when it eventually pays for it as a cash disbursement shown on the Cash Flow Statement.

FASB, the Financial Accounting Standards Board is a private, nonprofit organization made up of Certified Public Accountants (*CPAs*) whose purpose is to develop generally accepted accounting principles (*GAAP*), standards of financial accounting and reporting.

Inventory can be valued in two different ways depending on when the particular widget was manufactured and placed in the company's inventory: "FIFO" means "first-in; first-out." See *LIFO.*

With the effects of inflation, FIFO inventory valuation results in higher COGS and thus lower profits. FIFO valuation is a conservative accounting practice.

Financial statements are summaries and structured presentations of the various events (business transactions) that affect a company's financial performance.

Net fixed assets on the Balance Sheet, also called "property, plant & equipment" or PPE, is valued at historical cost (purchase price) less (net) an annual charge called *depreciation* that attempts to account for loss in value of the asset over time.

GHI

General & administrative expense (G&A) is a catch all including management, accounting, and other general business expenses.

"Generally Accepted Accounting Principles" are written standards of financial accounting and reporting for guidance and education of the public, including issuers, auditors, and other users of financial information. GAAP is promulgated by FASB.

The general ledger is a chronological listing, by account, of the details of every financial transaction of the company.

Gross Margin is the percentage of company's revenue that exceeds its cost of goods sold. It measures the ability of a company to generate revenue from the costs involved in production.

$$Gross\ Margin = \frac{Revenue - COGS}{Revenue}$$

Income means the same as earnings, profits (losses), or the "bottom-line." Income comes in two flavors, pre-tax (PBT or EBT) and after-tax (PAT).

The Income Statement (P&L) shows for an accounting period, the manufacturing and selling transactions that result in profit or loss.

Inventory is products ready for sale to clients, work-in-process (unfinished products still being manufactured), and any raw materials on-hand for making into products later. Inventory values, which also include manufacturing labor costs, will be turned into cost-of-goods-sold on the Income Statement when sold and delivered to a customer.

Inventory turn measures the level of business that can be conducted with a given investment in inventory. The lower the inventory relative to sales, the better.

$$Inventory\ Turn = \frac{COGS}{Inventory}$$

Inventory Valuation
See FIFO and LIFO.

JKL

A journal is a record of financial transactions in order by date. A journal is often defined as the book of original entry.

An element of inventory value represented by the cost of labor required to manufacture the product.

MNOP

Oreo is a brand of cookie consisting of two chocolate wafers with a sweet crème filling. Introduced in the year 1912 by the National Biscuit Company (now known as Nabisco), Oreo is the bestselling cookie in the world. Commemorating its original trademark date, Oreo Cookie Day is celebrated in the United States each year on March 6th.

One Oreo cookie (11.3g) has 53 calories and contains 2.3g fat, 8.3g carbohydrate, and 0.3g of protein, and hardly any vitamins.

If every Oreo cookie ever made (450 billion) were stacked on top of each other, the pile would reach to the moon and back more than six times.

QTRS

TUV

"Top Line"
See *Sales.*

Transaction 3

A transaction is any event that transfers money to or from the company, or transfers goods and services to or from the company. Transactions can also include new future financial obligations that the company assumes, or financial rights that the company is granted from others.

WXYZ

Worth, Net 15

Net Worth is the amount by which assets exceed liabilities. It is the value of everything you own, minus all your debts. Net worth is a concept that can be applied to both individuals and businesses, as a measure of how much they are really worth.

Well, that's all folks! Have a slice of pie or a bunch of cookies (or both). You have earned them!

The *World Wide Web* is a very valuable reference resource to use for understanding financial reporting topics. Both **Wikipedia** and **Investopia** are particularly informative, useful sites. Write a search with an accounting term and add *Wikipedia* or *Investopia* to be directed to the topic URL on their respective sites.

Notes:

_____

_____

_____

_____

_____

_____

_____

_____

_____

_____

_____

_____

_____

_____

_____

_____

_____

_____

_____

_____

Acknowledgements

I dedicate this book to my son Alasdair, who has had the good sense to become a lawyer and not an accountant. Also to Barbie and to Joe.

———

Many people helped make this book a reality. First and foremost, thanks to my family: Mary, Johnny, Bobbi, Darcy, Sara & Tim, Brenden, Bryce, and baby Callie for being on my side, at my side.

Thanks to Izzy Stemp who first taught me that accounting was nothing to fear.

Thanks to Ron Fry of Career Press who 20 years ago saw promise in my first financial statements manuscript and agreed to publish it. Now with over 200,000 copies in print, we certainly forged a productive partnership.

Many thanks to my editor Kate Osthaus CPA, for making my words flow and my numbers correct. However, I take full responsibility for errors and misstatements that remain. They are my own. Sigh.

My thanks to Karen Rivard, Esq and Sallie Randolph, Esq for keeping me out of jail, to Elizabeth Ames for strategic counsel, to Jean-Ann Schulte for her careful manuscript review, to Drs. Leann Canty and Rachel Fawcett for keeping me healthy, to Barbarajo Bockenhauer for her valuable conceptual editing of manuscript drafts and her continuing encouragement and heckling, to Gwen Acton for her content and format ideas and for help to keep me sane (mostly), to David Reid for sending me laughs, to Stacia O'Neil for trips to the New Hampshire coast, and to Stephen J. Potter for calling me from the road.

———

Finally, thanks to Paul O'Brian and the Tuesday morning crew, God bless them, every one.

Three new books in this series available soon on Amazon:

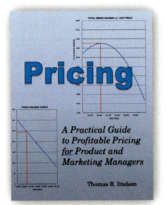

Pricing: A Practical Guide to Profitable Pricing for Product and Marketing Managers

Thomas R. Ittelson, Mercury Group Press, 2019 *(40 pages)*

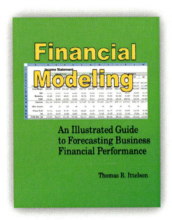

Financial Modeling: An Illustrated Guide to Forecasting Business Financial Performance

Thomas R. Ittelson, Mercury Group Press, 2019 *(40 pages)*

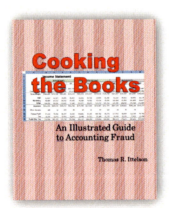

Cooking the Books: An Illustrated Guide to Accounting Fraud

Thomas R. Ittelson, Mercury Group Press, 2019 *(40 pages)*

MERCURY GROUP PRESS
PO BOX 381350
CAMBRIDGE, MA 02238
617-285-1168
INFO@MERCURYGROUP.COM

About the Author

Dear Readers,

I come to accounting through the laboratory, a kind of circuitous route to travel for sure. Armed with my formal training as a PhD-level natural scientist, I was working in a biotechnology lab. My main task was pouring liquid from Test Tube A into the liquid in Test Tube B, shaking and measuring how long it took the mixture to turn blue. I got bored (who would not?) and started a high tech company instead, learning accounting on the job.

My own "lightning bolt" moment during that learning process? Professional accountants, while very useful in performing audits, had great difficulty teaching me key accounting principles. I am a smart guy, but I consistently became mired in the specialized vocabulary and buried by what seemed unnecessary detail.

Being a scientist *and* a businessperson, I recognized a problem and wrote the book to solve it, my 285-page textbook for non-financial managers in companies. It is a popular text, with over 200,000 copies in print. Buy it if you want more accounting details than are in this picture book.

Financial Statements: A Step-by-Step Guide to Understanding & Creating Financial Reports, Second Edition
Career Press, 2009 ISBN: 978-1-60163-023-0

photo by Ralph Brown

I am a for-profit businessperson, but my recent work with nonprofit organizations led me to recognize that non-financial nonprofit board members, managers and staff all require a simple working knowledge of accounting and financial statements to do their charitable works. My two new nonprofit books have come from this interest. See the listings on the **Table of Contents** page for details.

Email me with any questions you have. I'm happy to help.

My best,

Cambridge, Massachusetts

ittelson@mercurygroup.com

Notes:

_____

_____

_____

_____

_____

_____

_____

_____

_____

_____

_____

_____

_____

_____

_____

_____

_____

_____

_____

_____

_____

_____

_____

_____

_____

_____

_____

_____

_____

_____

_____

_____

_____

_____

_____

_____

_____

_____

MERCURY GROUP PRESS • P.O. BOX 381350 • CAMBRIDGE, MASSACHUSETTS 02238 • INFO@MERCURYGROUP.COM

Made in United States
Orlando, FL
12 December 2024